Praise for Kenneth Steven

Evensong (2011)

'This collection of poems by Kenneth Steven is
stunning. There is a grave beauty in these lines,
revealing a poetic voice of great sensitivity. These
poems are, quite simply, wonderful'
ALEXANDER MCCALL SMITH

'For those of us who know Scotland, though not as natives,
and for those of us who are forever attempting to know
ourselves, Kenneth Steven is another inner voice, and
never more so than in this collection of his work.
Evensong is intimate and beautiful'
RONALD BLYTHE

The Ice and Other Stories (2010)

'Beautiful, enchanting, heartbreaking'
CHRIS DOLAN

'*The Ice* is an atmospheric, wintry tale of fragile human
relationships set in a beautiful but unforgiving landscape'
JAMES ROBERTSON

'*The Ice* comes straight out a tradition running through Neil
Gunn and Robin Jenkins – precise, sweetly written, slow-
moving and with a melancholy air in an uncontrived style'
DES DILLON

'A wonderful short story writer – a very beautiful, enjoyable
collection from a multi-talented writer'
OSPREY JOURNAL

Imagining Things (2005)

'Enjoying your work intensely – style and subject'
TED HUGHES

'Strong a

A

A Note on the Author

Kenneth Steven was born in Glasgow in 1968 and spent his schooldays in Perthshire. He has studied in Norway and translates from both Norwegian and Sami. A widely published poet, novelist and children's author, his most recently published collections of poetry include *Evensong*, *Iona* and *Wild Horses*. His translation of Laars Saaybe Christensen's *The Half Brother* was a finalist for the 2004 *Independent* Foreign Fiction Prize. He travels widely to give readings and writing workshops for both adults and youngsters. He lives in Dunkeld with his family.

A Song among the Stones

KENNETH STEVEN

Au best wishes,

Kenn Steven

Polygon

First published in Great Britain in 2012 by Polygon,
an imprint of Birlinn Ltd
West Newington House
10 Newington Road
Edinburgh
EH9 1QS
www.birlinn.co.uk

ISBN: 978 1 84697 7 212 6

British Library Cataloguing-in-Publication Data
A catalogue record for this book is available on
request from the British Library.

Typeset in Great Britain by Antony Gray
Printed and bound by TJ International Ltd, Padstow, Cornwall

for my mother,
and to remember my father,
who taught me to walk on Iona

Preface

In the sixth century, Celtic Christians monks are likely to have made the journey from Iona to Iceland and the Faeroe Islands. In later centuries, the Norse settlers who made their homes in the Western and Northern Isles of Scotland found evidence of stone chapels and cross slabs; the Christian hermits who built these were known to the Norse as the 'papar'.

To this day, the papar presence is remembered in the names the settlers gave to the islands, such as Pabbay, Papadil and Papa Westray. The early Celtic church appears to have been accepted without any real resistance by the people of Ireland. When the Christian gospel travelled across the water to what we know today as Galloway and Argyll, the story was the same. But the Celtic monks were well aware that the first Christians had suffered all manner of persecution for their faith; they knew that faith had gone hand in glove with suffering, and often with martyrdom.

Setting out on journeys of faith to reach the wild coasts of Ireland and Scotland, to build chapels there and to seek God in the very teeth of the storm was a kind of martyrdom. While these places had neither deserts nor roaring lions, there were tempestuous seas and seemingly numberless dangerous rocks and small islands to navigate.

Iona was the heart of the Celtic Christian world in the sixth century. Columba had made the island his home and his abbey had been build there. At that time, Iona wasn't remote in the way we might consider it today; it lay in the middle of the sea roads, and in Columba's day it was a busy, vibrant hub of religious teaching and thinking, likely to have been the place where the Book of Kells, the great treasure of the Celts, was begun.

Perhaps in the end, it became too loud and cluttered for the hermits, who yearned for solitude and complete wilderness in their search for the divine. They went further and further into the sea 'desert' to find the empty places for which they longed. On the east coast of Iceland, there is a tiny island by the name of Papey. The Norse settlers believed that this was a place visited by the Celtic hermits. Indeed, to this very day, Icelandic archaeologists continue to scour Papey for proof of some kind of early Christian settlement. All it would take to confirm this would be a single cross-marked slab.

What I love about this story is the absence of written history: time allows the imagination freedom to move and breathe. In so many places, the human story encompasses every footfall and sentence; Papey's history offers the possibility of an extraordinary journey, neither more nor less. It is an elemental story, as sparse and weathered as one of those last poems by the great Orcadian, George Mackay Brown.

It is my intention and hope that the following sequence of poems be read as one unbroken piece, in a re-creation of the papar journey itself, from the west coast of Scotland to Iceland. I have sought to give the sense of the fragments of some lost manuscript, found perhaps centuries later on Iona, and now nothing more than the last worn-away stones of the story.

KS

A SONG AMONG THE STONES

the water lilies pearling the lochs
ruffled in the tugging of the wind

the sunlight comes wild and strong
in gusts like bunches of blown daffodils

this northernness novembered in a moment
driven slate-grey in a suddenness of storm

yet this is the place they came to find
an island thin to the divine

on the edge of the world
a beauty brittle as a bird's egg

larks spinning songs out of sheer sky
orchids blowing in hidden glens

and sometimes, just sometimes
the glory of God in the morning

the light lay in all the fields
and the curlews wept in the blue wind

they walked in rhythm through the fields
as though hearing a song that was not there

a man kissed his son's head
and led him slowly, slowly home

and the bell held in the still air
slow and long in evensong

up in the winds of the tower
all day, all night
pen and nib and ink
yellows and reds and blues
poured into every page
this gospel of love of God

outside, the bones of winter
rattle all night long
the sea struggling
rolling in its sleep, fevered
as the waves break in shining
on this shattered western edge

in the small hours they gathered
up under the roof of the tower
there where the book was being brought
beautiful, out of nowhere

they watched him, wary, wondering –
I am going further north, he said
I do not know what I will find
perhaps I will not come back

all I know is that I must seek
this somewhere with all my soul

a day out of clean silk
washed like a child that's lived for days
in fever, the light pure and perfect
and nothing troubled left in all the world

a day to love a neighbour
to see in the young field's promise
God rippling and strong, unquestionable

four men gathered from the island
went down to the shore
ready for the vessel, eyes full and wide

and the moon rose over the rim of the earth
and fell like fish upon the sea
their moon road north

islands of sea, floors of sea
valleys of sea, hills of sea
lifts of sea, slopes of sea
peaks of sea, rafts of sea
hollows of sea, steeps of sea
descents of sea, edges of sea
channels of sea, pieces of sea
searches of sea, darkenings of sea
flickerings of sea, glimpses of sea
layers of sea, shapes of sea
shapes of sea, shapes of sea

the youngest woke alone

they were curled into the boat
faces blue-white with the night

the last of the land was leaving them
north waited, watching

why had he come
was it for God, or for the girl on the island
whose eyes smiled when she passed every dawn
on her way to the well

was it for her

the sea rose and fell
a dark breath

was that a light
who lived there

he looked, leaning out
yearning for answers

all he knew was a sore fear
goring him

he held onto the light
like a child

tell us a story, they said

he thought a long time
unsure, like someone
searching blind in a cave

these are pieces of story, he said
like the charred ends of burned wood
and odd glow of ember
lighting like an eye when blown

Sunniva, an Irish princess
lusted after by some chieftain thug
fled with her followers
across the sea into fragments of islands
blown wherever God would

into the gnarled edges of western Norway
in and out of storm
a place driven by flocks of snow
a blue wind all summer

in time they heard whisperings of her again
sought to root her out as a bear
claws wild honey from a stump

she prayed the rocks might fall
rather than be carried off alive
buried under mountain rubble

however many years after
in the half darkness of winter
they came to Selja, saw strange light
glowing underneath the rocks

there the monastery was built
of broken stone
above the place where she had never died

late in evening the sky bruised
ringed them ugly and full
the sea moiled, black with heaving
feverish and wild

the rimless sky flickered with lightning
thunder padded and prowled
the wind woke, came like a beast
pawing this way and that

and the boat plunged and heaved
they held on in the scream of the sea
praying that as Christ had once calmed them
the waters might hear him again

then one of them looked and saw
in the midst of the worst of the night
a star chinking like gold
he pointed, they followed his arm

the storm did not lessen the least
but their faith was made of new fire
they fought like men unafraid
and the morning was born at last

the youngest dreamed of Ireland
warm with hay, safe, a place
to lie and snug among the softness
rocked by sleep

the up-in-the-morning early light
the buttercup fields knee-deep in sun
the woods splayed with yellow patches,
birdsong

the running laughter of the river
until the soft fall of night

the breath of the blue trees
the cloth call of an owl

another dreamed of Noah, how
through the heavy grapes of rain
the dove brought in its beak
the tiniest chink of light

another dreamed they were following a strange cloud
that they left everything behind
even their own names

the eyes of those they met
searching

they clutched children to themselves
like hunger, stared like strange moons
whose dead seas tide no longer

at night they dreamed of who they were
and wakened wondering

the last did not sleep at all
for fear of what he might dream

they thirsted, water all around them
mouths grew ugly, black and bulged

they muttered darkness in their sleep
and woke with ash in their mouths

they leered out over the sea
starving for land, nothing but hills of ripples
silence huge in their heads

and on the third morning
it grew out of the fronds of mist
like some broken bird, ungreened and gaunt

a rock in the bare sea

they went ashore like ghosts
feet bashed and bruised, and then
water spoke in tongues, burst
up from the stone floor, they fell
like beasts to lap their fill

it was God who sent us here, one said
closing his eyes

no, said another, it was the island
that was sent by God to find us

look, someone said
there's a light on the sea
and they turned, clumsy and slow
mouths scabbed, dry-caked gashes
in their faces, their hands
like thumped lumps of fishes
bloodied and sore with cold
their eyes faraway, slow
deep in the bones of their faces

not a light at all
an eye of red smouldering the sea
north and north of north
a wound of blood and pus

all night it enflamed the sky
throbbing the dark and rumbling
like some ancient raging beast

they lay awake, watching
an unblinking in their eyes
and the mountain rose up smoking

land lay at anchor
a ledge of darkness

the sea swivelled
hissed in its rolling

the boat lurched and swung
like thread through the eye of a needle

closer and closer
into a cut in the cliffs

the stench of birds and wet stone
the rocks a singing of droplets

they crouched, salt-lipped
their mouths dry caves

the dank slap of water
the thick, bad air

and the boat nudged in
dunted a black beach

that night she awoke
knowing

she dressed in the stone darkness
went out barefoot

into the bright wind
a silvering of clouds

down and down she went
hurrying her heart

until she reached at last
the monastery's sleep

her feet soft as swallow's wings
slipping the stone steps

he gathered her in his arms
searched her wild eyes

they're safe, she said, I'm certain
I have seen them in my sleep

for two days they slept, dreamless
and the sea breathed beyond them
like the sea a child hears in a shell

then the one who'd brought them there
woke, went out of the cave in bare feet
into a land without a name

he stood and looked, a waterfall
like the galloping of a thousand white horses
leapt over the edge of a cliff

a mountain
smoke drifting from its shoulders
bleeding from a deep wound in its head

and beyond, a silence
vast as the sky
reaching the very edge of the light

he bent to the broken rocks
rose a cross with his bare hands

they built somewhere out of burnt stone
a beehive that let in pieces of sky

all day they bore stones
boulders heavy as themselves

inside it felt like a child's secret
dark and soft and warm

and after day came a strangeness
night that was not night at all

the sky deepened blue and pure
the hills stared white and still

the air filled with an evensong of birds
a sorrowing of voices, seen and unseen

a melding of many things
and they lay there listening

they called it the house of peace
wove songs and prayers into the walls

until it became a safeness, a sanctuary

two of them crouched
by a silver dance of river

sometimes faith is elusive
hard to catch as a fish

God is distant and brittle
as a star on the night's edge

sometimes everything seems
desolate as a winter land

so what is left then
asked the youngest, turning

to remember this
said the one who brought them

a golden crook of lightning
fluttered from the sky
and lit a stable

the youngest was restless
went looking

all day and all night he walked
and the sun grew full and orange

birds sang over lakes
their voices beautiful echoes

trailing in the open emptiness
a long and eerie sadness

he walked until he feared
he would not find his way back

and he remembered one in Ireland
who said he heard angels singing

his face made of shining
sure and brilliant with light

who left and never came back
to search for what he had heard

was that what God asked
was that the highest gift

or was it a kind of madness
an imagining set alight

the youngest remembered him
mile after mile after mile

he heard song
but it was nothing more than the birds

and he wondered as he went
if he feared to find God too great

one day
the youngest spoke and could not look at them

I miss the warm bread
broken in the morning

I miss the cloister
with the wind in the grass

I miss the curragh
coming full to the brim with word of Ireland

I miss the voices of women
the kind softness of their talk

I miss the books and their pages
the scent of leather

I miss everything I cannot have
and my prayers have grown thin and bitter

I ask that we may go back home

but the one who'd brought them there
did not come with them

they turned to look at him, it seemed
as if they stood below, in shadow

I won't go with you. Tell them I stayed
that I went further north, to what I cannot know
but this is what I want
I'm closer than I was, I'm almost there

the youngest thought
his words were almost song
his face bright and shining silver

they watched him, dumb
as even then he turned away
began his journey

and a mist grew about them
blew in from the edges of the sea
a low hiss of nothingness
wrapping them in its wool

hour after hour the sea never moved
lay eerie and still
they waited, watching, not talking
hair filled with glistenings of rain

and one by one
they crept into the edges of the boat
slept where they sat, heads bent
rocked in the somewhere of the sea

he imagined the girl with the golden hair
swimming that early morning

over on the west, in the dark green deep
of the pool breathed by the ocean

and coming back, her footprints silver
through the thin and windswept grass

sunlight flickering the fields
as a hand ripples a harp

the clink of the bell gathering the brothers
the soft murmur of their voices

and he did not know if it was better
to dream or really to be there

they held the monastery in their eyes
beloved, the most beautiful gift
between the broken fragments
of sea and sky and land

a song among the stones

Acknowledgments

The roots of *A Song among the Stones* lie in a commission by BBC Radio 3; segments first written for *The Verb* were broadcast on the programme. Individual pieces of the sequence then went on to be published in *Sofia*, *The Merton Journal*, *Coracle*, *Acumen* and *Other Poetry*. The sequence as a whole was published by *Poetry Scotland*.

A grant from Dumfries and Galloway Arts Association allowed the Scottish clarsach exponent Wendy Stewart to compose a sequence of pieces to flow through and between the words. The resulting work was recorded and was performed in the village of Moniaive in Dumfriesshire.

The composer John Hearne, who hails from the north-east of Scotland and has long-standing connections with Iceland, used the sequence in the creation of a choral work. This was first performed by the Stonehaven Chorus on 27 May 2012.